MIRACLES

9 God Stories Told by Kids

by Patricia A. Frost

Illustrations by Emily Naylor

MIRACLES
Copyright © 2020 by Patricia A. Frost
Illustrated by Emily Naylor

Printed in Canada

Print ISBN: 978-1-4866-1942-9
eBook ISBN: 978-1-4866-1943-6

Word Alive Press
119 De Baets Street, Winnipeg, MB R2J 3R9
www.wordalivepress.ca

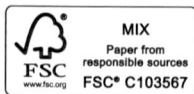

WORD ALIVE
—P R E S S—

FSC
www.fsc.org

MIX
Paper from
responsible sources
FSC® C103567

Cataloguing in Publication may be obtained through Library and Archives Canada

ANNA

and

EMMA

You don't have to be an adult to see Jesus do a ☺ miracle ☺.
Let me tell you my story.

Hello!

My name is Anna. I am six years old and in Grade One. I live with my mommy and daddy and my older sister, Emma. I want to tell you some things Jesus did for me.

I was so **confused**! There I was, six years old and full of a million questions. My mom was acting strange—very strange—and I had to know why. She was so much happier than usual, and she even ♫ sang ♫ while she worked! I loved it. But why was this happening? And what was that book she read so much? Why was she always talking about Jesus?

My mommy told me that Jesus loved me so much, He left heaven and was born to Mary. (God was His daddy.) He grew up and played like I do with my friends. As a man, He did many ☺ miracles ☺. He died on the † cross † for me and rose ☼ again after three days.

Mommy told me that if I asked Jesus to come live in my heart and put my trust in Him, He would save me. If I made Him my Lord and Saviour, I would have an *exciting* life.

My mom, Emma, and I prayed. Jesus came to live in my heart at that very moment! Then everything changed.

Our home became very different. We *laughed* more and had so much fun. We ♫ sang ♫ songs about Jesus. We read the Bible and learned about the *exciting* things that Jesus did.

Then God started showing us His power. The ☺ **miracles** ☺ **started happening ...**

"They replied, 'Believe in the Lord Jesus and you will be saved, along with everyone in your household'."
—Acts 16:31

* * *

EMMA
and the Sick
HAMSTER

Emma and I were playing with some kids when one of the boys asked if we would like two baby hamsters. We **jumped** for joy at the thought of having two new pets. We put them in an aquarium on the floor at the end of the hall. Over the next few days, we spent every spare minute watching our new pets run on their wheel. We fed them sunflower seeds and held them. One afternoon, I noticed that Emma's hamster had a sore eye, so I picked it up and **prayed** for God to heal its eye in Jesus's name.

I don't know why Mom didn't pray. She just wanted to get medicine for the hamster. Two days later, she noticed the little pet's eye had healed, **even** without the medicine! Mom asked if I had 𝔭𝔯𝔞𝔶𝔢𝔡 for the hamster. When I told her that I had, she told me that its eye was healed, and we praised God together. **God really does care for every part of our lives.**

"Ask, and you will receive, that your joy may be full."
—John 16:24b, NKJV

* * *

ANNA

and the

BLIZZARD

One day, I was sitting in what is usually a noisy classroom, but that day I didn't hear a sound. I was thinking about the ❄ **BLIZZARD** ❄ raging outside the classroom.

As I looked out the window, **shivers** ran up and down my spine. The snow was falling so heavily, it looked like a white blanket over the window. When the wind blew, the blanket of snow parted just enough to see the drifts of snow on the street. Soon I would be walking right into the **FIERCE WIND** and blinding snow. Oh, how I **shivered** when I thought about that!

What had I heard at church? In Genesis it says that we have dominion (power) over the weather. I also remembered the time Elijah told the rain to stop, and it did. As little butterflies started jumping in my stomach, I thought that maybe I could tell that storm to stop, and it would have to listen to me. So that is what I did. I told the storm to **leave now** in Jesus's name. Wind **stop** blowing! Snow **stop** falling in Jesus's name! I quickly went back to work and didn't think about the storm again until the bell rang.

> *"Yes, ask me for anything in my name, and I will do it!"*
>
> —John 14:14

I was so excited when I walked out the school door and saw that the ❄ **BLIZZARD** ❄ had stopped. There wasn't a breath of wind, and the sun was peeking out of the clouds. It seemed to have a twinkle in its eye and be saying, "Praise God." **He even answers the prayers of a six-year-old**.

Do you know that Jesus answers **all** of my prayers? He will answer yours too.

"And God said ... let them have dominion ... over all the earth..."

—Genesis 1:26, KJV

* * *

EMMA

and the Loose

TOOTH

Have you ever had a wiggly tooth? Did you pull it out, or did you let it get so loose it just fell out?

One day, Grandma, Mom, Emma, and I went to a fancy hotel to water slide and swim. Emma had a very loose tooth. Every time I looked at her, she was wiggling it to see if she could pull it out.

We were so excited about going for a water slide and swim! We grabbed our towels and headed for the elevator. No talk now of a wiggly tooth, just thoughts of *whizzing* down the slide into the cool water! We threw down our towels and climbed up the steps of the slide while Mommy and Grandma watched. Up and down we went, giggling and splashing.

All of a sudden, I noticed Emma's tooth was gone. Now, where should we look for that lost tooth? Without even thinking, we bowed our heads and asked Jesus to show us the lost tooth. This might seem strange to you, but we were sure that the Lord would show us the missing tooth.

We dove into the water, searched the deck, and shook our towels. No tooth was to be found. We couldn't believe that Jesus hadn't shown us the tooth, but we had to quit looking because it was time to go and get ready for supper. We ☹ sadly ☹ picked up our towels, got on the elevator, and went back to our room.

As soon as we got back into the hotel room, Emma started combing her hair. All of a sudden, I let out a **squeal**. You guessed it. There on the floor was the missing tooth! Only an ✼ angel ✼ of God could have tucked it into Emma's hair. God was true to His Word and answered our 𝔭𝔯𝔞𝔶𝔢𝔯.

"I also tell you this: If two of you agree here on earth concerning anything you ask, my Father in heaven will do it for you."

—Matthew 18:19

* * *

EMMA

and the Toboggan

RIDE

"What a beautiful day for a toboggan ride!" exclaimed Dad. So off we went to the hills for the afternoon. It was indeed a gorgeous day as Emma and I ran up the hills and *giggled* all the way down on our toboggans. We had lots of laughs until we hit a **bump** and went *FLYING* through the air. That was the end of the rides that day, as Emma had hurt her knee and could barely limp back to the car.

That evening we sat around the table praising the Lord. One of our favorite songs was "He Touched Me." As we were singing that song to the Lord, Emma stood up to get a drink. As she walked across the floor, I noticed she was no longer limping. In a split second, she let out a **squeal**. She knew beyond any doubt that while she had been singing to Jesus, He had reached down and touched her.

Oh, **Jesus is so wonderful!** He really has kept His promises and given us an *exciting* life. Some other kids have stories they would like to tell you.

"And these signs will follow those who believe..."
—Mark 16:17a, NKJV

SHEENA
and Her
DOLL

Hi, my name is Sheena, and I want to tell you about some of the most wonderful things Jesus did for my brother and me.

When I was five years old, I went to the lake with Mommy and Daddy and my brother, Clark. While Mommy and Daddy were playing volleyball, I was sitting on the sand with Teresa, my **most favorite** doll in the whole world. She came all the way across the ocean from Germany. I tucked her into her bed in my gym bag and left her on the beach while I ran to talk to Mommy and Daddy. I was so *excited* about the volleyball game, I forgot all about Teresa and left her on the beach all night.

In the morning, I discovered that I had forgotten Teresa. I ran back to the beach to find her, but she was gone!

We put up signs everywhere, but when Mommy and Daddy's holidays were over, we had to go back home without Teresa. I felt very ☹ sad ☹. That night I prayed with my mommy and daddy. I told (commissioned) my 🕊 angels 🕊 to keep my doll safe and bring her back to me.

The next summer when I was six, we went back to the same beach. Mommy and Daddy and I had been praying every night, asking Jesus to look after Teresa and send His ✞ angels ✞ to bring her safely home to me. Again, she was nowhere to be found, and again we had to leave the beach without Teresa.

On my seventh birthday, Mommy came to pick me up at school. She said, "I know we still pray for God to bring Teresa home, but do you believe He will?"

I answered, "Oh yes, Mommy, I know He will."

Then my mommy opened the trunk of the car, and there was my gym bag with Teresa safe inside. I grabbed Teresa and hugged and hugged her. I was so **excited**. I couldn't wait to tell all my friends that **Jesus had answered my prayers.**

Jesus had kept my doll and my gym bag safe until someone found her. The forest ranger had found the gym bag, and when he looked inside, he saw my doll and also our name and address. He drove all the way to our city and brought her to our house that very day. **Thank you, Jesus**.

"I waited patiently for the Lord to help me, and he turned to me and heard my cry."

—Psalm 40:1

* * *

CLARK

and His Special

KNIFE

My brother Clark doesn't play with dolls, but he had a ☺ miracle ☺ just like mine. When he was eleven, he had a very special knife. It was a Swiss Army knife. It was red with silver and a cross on it. It cost him over fifty dollars.

Clark was playing tennis with three of his friends. His knife kept falling out of his pocket and dragging on the cement, so he took it and set it down by the post and finished his game.

After the game, he and his friends left the beach, *chatting excitedly*, so he forgot about his knife. That's my brother!

Three hours later he reached for his knife on his belt loop. When he discovered that it wasn't there, he remembered setting it down by the post, so he ran quickly to get it. How horrible! It wasn't there! Who would have taken his special Swiss Army knife? We asked everyone if they had seen the knife. We even offered a twenty-dollar reward if they found it.

Just like I had *prayed* for Teresa, Clark prayed that God would bring his knife back safely with no marks on it or the blade. Clark knew that if Jesus had answered my prayers, He would also answer his. Clark was **BOLD LIKE A LION** in his prayers. The next two nights he prayed with his three friends. In the morning, when Clark was in the yard, he looked up and saw a strange man coming towards him. Clark wondered who the man was and why he was visiting us.

His curiosity turned to **excitement** when the man held up a red Swiss Army knife. He didn't get a chance to ask his question before Clark shouted, "**You found my lost knife!**"

The man asked, "Are you sure that it's your knife?"

Clark happily said that it was. We offered him the twenty-dollar reward, but the man wouldn't take it. He just told Clark to be more careful. The knife was in the same great condition that it was in when he'd lost it. Not one new scratch on it. He thanked God for that—lots.

"Don't worry about anything; instead, pray about everything. Tell God what you need, and thank him for all he has done"

—Philippians 4:6

* * *

DONNA
and the
BUGS

Hi, my name is Donna. When I was only two years old, my grandma tucked me into bed one night. She said to me, "Sleep tight and don't let the bed bugs **BITE**." I thought there really were bugs that were going to bite me!

A few nights later, when my mom was tucking me into bed, I kicked the covers off, and she covered me up again. Then I kicked the covers off again.

"Why do you keep kicking off the covers?" she asked.

I told her that I didn't want the bed MONsters that Grandma had told me about biting me. Mom got out her Bible and read me the scripture that says not to fear because God is with me. Then I wasn't afraid any more.

"For God has not given us a spirit of fear and timidity, but of power, love, and self-discipline."
—2 Timothy 1:7

ROBBIE

and the

RACES

My name is Robbie, and I am twelve years old. I love to run in races. At the end of the racing season last year, I got **very, very** sick. I would get really **HOT** and then really *COLD*. My head ached, and I'd felt so dizzy. I didn't want to eat at all, which is very strange for a twelve-year-old! I could hardly get off the couch.

The doctors didn't know what was wrong with me. I really wanted Jesus to heal me, because I had worked so hard and had dreamed of running all these races. Twice I even convinced Mom and Dad that I was better just so I could run, but after those races I was weaker and worse than before. There was one more **big**, **big** race left—the

Provincials. Mom and Dad said that I couldn't run unless I got a ☺ miracle ☺.

I listened to Scriptures from the Bible about how Jesus went about healing people until I was like a sponge full of God's Word. After I had listened many times, I decided that I could be healed too. So I got up and began praying and walking back and forth. After about ten minutes, I felt a *cool wind* come over me, and it took away all the sickness. I was healed! Then I kept praying for about an hour and a half. I mostly said, "By His stripes I was healed." I prayed in tongues and thanked God for His healing.

Later, when Mom came into the room, she could tell immediately that I was healed. I phoned my dad at work to tell him that Jesus had healed me. As soon as I told Dad, he said that he could tell I was healed just by the sound of my voice.

That night we had yummy pizza for supper—my favorite! I really did get my ☺ miracle ☺. I was so excited, because I got to run in the Provincials. What a great way to end the racing season—*to be healed by Jesus*.

The sickness tried to come back twice after that, but we prayed each time and it went away.

"who Himself bore our sins in His own body on the tree, that we, having died to sins, might live for righteousness—by whose stripes you were healed."
—1 Peter 2:24, NKJV

* * *

NOTE FROM THE AUTHOR

These are just a few stories that children have shared with me. Jesus wants to do ☺ miracles ☺ for you also. **If you do what these children did, you will get your ☺ miracles! ☺**
Find a scripture.
Ask the Father in Jesus's name.
Believe He will do it.
Thank God and worship Him until you see the answer.

> *"And whatever things you ask in prayer, believing, you will receive."*
>
> —Matthew 21:22, NKJV

DRAW

a Picture of Your

MIRACLE